Bullying

BY DEREK O'NEILL

Derek O'Neill
244 5th Avenue, Suite D-264
New York, NY 10001
E-Mail: info@derekoneill.com

ISBN: 978-1-936470-57-0
First Edition

Get a Grip Series © 2016
Editor: Nancy Moss
Front Cover Design: Derek O'Neill

DEDICATION

To all who read this book, I salute you for wanting to change the way you live for the better and for having the courage to be who you are as fully as possible.

To all who encourage me everyday to keep going and sharing their lives with me, family small and large. But most of all the little angels who came to teach me – Alexa and Blake, my grandchildren.

"Everybody hurts sometimes, and when we do it is nice to have Derek O'Neill around. His excellent little books on the things that get us, (fear, anger, depression, victimhood, mental blocks) allow us to find our way safely through our psychological minefields and arrive safely at the other side. Read them when you need them."

Paul Perry, Author of the
New York Times Bestseller
Evidence of the Afterlife

AUTHOR'S PREFACE

Thank you for purchasing *Bullying: You won't beat me*. This book has not come about as a result of my training as a therapist, but through some hard-earned lessons that I have experienced myself. This is how I know the path out of limiting beliefs and behaviors that hinder growth. The tools that I offer in this book have worked not only for me, but also for hundreds if not thousands of other people. I have shared these ideas and techniques in my workshops, one-on-one sessions, video and radio broadcasts, and on my website, and I have witnessed astounding results time and time again. Through observation of others, and myself, I have learned to identify the triggers and root causes of disharmony. Most of all, I have come to understand and apply the best methods for achieving peace and balance in life; not perfection, but real transformation and harmony that comes with learning who we are and what makes us tick. My 35 years of martial arts study has given me a refined sense of timing for when to strike with the sword to cut away old patterns, and when to use the brush to paint the picture of the life we deserve and can have.

The 'Get a Grip' series of books offers tangible, authentic wisdom that can help you in all aspects of your life. You've made a great choice by investing in this book. Enjoy the read, and take time to learn and apply the techniques. Let's change who we are together.

Derek

TABLE OF CONTENTS

THE MANY FACES OF BULLYING

Have you ever been bullied? Is there someone in your life right now who uses bullying tactics to feel powerful? Do *you* display any tendencies toward bullying others? How does bullying affect our lives, our communities and our world?

Bullying is certainly not a new phenomenon but we seem to live in a time when it has escalated. Fortunately, we also live in a time of more awareness and openness. When we can identify bullying, stand up to it, and set out to change its dynamic, we can begin to heal individually and globally. One of the most valuable messages I can give you before we begin this exploration of bullying is; **There is help, and there is hope. Bullying can stop.**

There are few people who have not experienced bullying at some point in their lives. Many have participated in bullying behavior themselves. My youth included being the target of bullying, along with changes in my own behavior as a reaction to it. The effects of bullying, for both the bully and the victim, can alter our true nature.

When you are bullied you may begin to hold back your feelings, develop debilitating fears, or even become aggressive yourself. Childhood bullying can leave mental - and sometimes physical - scars for life. In its worst-case scenario, we see it at the root of all too many suicidal feelings and actions. Bullying is usually a complicated mixture of abusive anger, resentment, lack of confidence and pain. When a bully acts out, there's always more than meets the eye. If we look not just at the victim, but also the bully with compassion, we gain insight and answers that can help everyone.

We find bullying in all kinds of dynamics and environments. Childhood bullying, especially in the early teen years, is common but doesn't end there. Adults sometimes experience bullying in the workplace. We see it in romantic and family relationships. Bullying can be pronounced and obvious, or much subtler and even hard to recognize. We need to be able to clearly define bullying when we are the target, when we see others at its receiving end, and when we engage in it ourselves. For the victim of bullying, seeking help with friends, professionals and/or the authorities is so important to healing and putting all the complex feelings and reactions into perspective.

In the pages that follow, I hope to provide you with an overview of how to identify bullying, a look into what creates a bully, strategies for dealing with bullying and reaching out for help, and the role that your subconscious can play in changing the energy and effect of bullying. We will also explore spiritual and meditative approaches to creating a mindful attitude that protects you from harm, and lends compassion and understanding to those in so much pain that they would hurt others. At the end of this book you will find a list of online resources for support.

CHILDHOOD BULLYING

Many children are bullied during their school years, often on a regular basis. Studies show that up to 25% of teens experience some kind of bullying. The effects are often devastating and long-lasting. Self-image and confidence can be shattered and the ability to trust severely damaged. If you grow up with bullying – whether it is directed at you or you see it happening in your family – you begin to develop a problem with knowing what is acceptable interaction and communication. Many adults still suffer the effects of being bullied as a child or teen.

Any child can fall victim to a bully. Children who do well in school, or stand out in a unique way, are sometimes targeted. Jealousies and the pressure to conform play a role. It is so important to nurture what makes a child who they are, no matter what form that takes. When they set out with a sense of acceptance from their own family, a child or teen who faces bullying will at least have this to call upon within themselves. It doesn't mean that dealing with a bully will be easy and not hurt, but when our children don't feel supported as they grow up, the challenges that they face will be all the more overwhelming. It cannot be stated enough; **Accept your child for who they are.**

It's highly unlikely that it will be obvious whether or not your child is being bullied. Teens especially, may keep abuse under wraps from parents. This comes from a combination of shame, fear, and the common teenage mindset that to involve parents or teachers is to provoke more bullying. As parents, friends, teachers and members of a community, we must become sensitive to the signs and signals that kids are being bullied.

We want our children to feel safe and strong. Knowing what is going on in their lives that could be harmful is a start.

Is there a significant change of behavior and/or mood of the child? Have they stopped being enthusiastic about something that brought them joy in the past? Do they seem depressed? Are they spending more time alone? Has their social group changed, seemingly for no reason? Do they want to stay home from school, or say they are sick more than before? Is your child asking you to pick them up from school to avoid walking home? Have you noticed any signs of physical abuse – bruises or other marks? All of these need to be looked into right away. Another sign could be a teen's sudden disinterest in appearance. If you have a child who generally kept themself neat and tidy, and now all of sudden just seems not to care, investigate further. When you see their enthusiasm and confidence start to slip and slide, it is a classic sign that bullying might be behind it. The more vigilant a parent or teacher is in spotting potential bullying, the better the chances are for intervention and stopping things from spinning out of control.

Though we live in a time more tolerant of differences than in the past, we obviously cannot sit back and deny that hatred, fueled by fear, does not exist. When kids are in middle school, their search for identity and the need to be accepted blows in like a storm! These can be some of the most difficult years of one's early teens. Social cliques are formed and create the potential for exclusion. LBGT youth are often the target of bullying, at a time in their lives when it is so important for them to feel support and protection. Cyberbullying, which we look at more closely in an upcoming section of this book, is especially fertile ground for all kids to fall victim to - or participate in - bullying.

In the past decade or so, there's been a rise of awareness in the school setting for the need of anti-bullying and anti-violence programs and policies. If your school doesn't have these resources and trainings, please get involved and see that they are implemented. It is a matter of children's safety and well-being. There's no excuse for each and every school, no matter the size and location, to not have these programs. Children need the schools and their parents to stand up for them - when they often cannot themselves - and provide the outreach they deserve.

Kids and teens will always find things in their peers to pick on them about. The bully will feel elevated and superior, though usually that's short-lived. It's important to address the child who is doing the bullying and dig deeper into their motivations. Healing is needed all-around. When we tell children that their bully lacks self-confidence or is jealous of them, it's not enough. We need to really attend to what is going on below the surface of each side of the equation so we can empower those affected and stop the patterns of abuse. Bullies are abusing themselves by their very acts, but this part of the puzzle often gets lost in the mix.

What creates a bully? A child can learn the behavior from their parents, even in subtle ways. Parents need to be aware of their influence. If you are sitting at the dinner table and make a derogatory remark about a certain race, religion, or creed, you're creating a bully. If you gossip about people, saying negative things and putting them down, you are planting the seed for a bully. Do you ever call your child names, tease them, berate or manipulate them? Don't be surprised to see them echo this behavior and carry it into adulthood. As children get older, some parents try to press them into choices about careers and other decisions they need to make, to be true to who they are. Please be vigilant to not bully young adults into what *you* want for them, rather than letting them find their own path.

WORKPLACE BULLYING

We spend a lot of our time in our work environments. It stands to reason that the dynamics of people interacting with one another under the pressure of expectations and goals is going to create disharmony from time to time. This is normal, but when someone begins to harass, badger, tease, start rumors, or make unwelcomed advances towards a co-worker, that is bullying plain and simple - and it must stop. The hierarchy of power in the workplace, along with jealousies, resentments, and emotion-fueled perceptions can all lead to someone being bullied.

Bullying in the workplace can range from threats, insults, or cruel reprimands to very subtle comments or actions that make you feel on edge. Someone might be taking credit for your work, or changing it. Are you being ignored or overlooked, over and over? Is someone continually disrespecting your time or asking for more than you are responsible for? If your boss is the bully, even if they aren't telling you verbally that your job is in jeopardy, you may feel you could lose your employment if you stand up to them or report them to their superior. The extra element of trying to do what is right for you, while needing to earn a living, can make workplace bullying a complicated issue. Often, people feel they cannot risk being back out in the world looking for a new job, especially in an economy which lacks choices. If the bullying continues, and continues to harm you, the price of remaining quiet can be high. Accepting bullying – unless it truly doesn't bother you – can affect your mental, physical and spiritual health.

If you are being bullied at work, chances are you are not the only victim of the bully.

Talk to coworkers and you may find out that you are not alone. Having allies can make you feel more grounded in your resolve to stand up to the bully and present a stronger case if you end up reporting the bullying to your higher-ups. If you wallow in feeling bad, you are giving bullies what they want – control. If you are being bullied by someone, take note of it. Write down where you were when it happened, if anyone else was there, and exactly what was said or what action transpired. If you need documentation or evidence down the line, you will have it.

It helps to approach workplace bullying with a mindful, whole-picture attitude. When you feel you are the target of a bully, try to look at the context. Is the company itself dysfunctional? Do the supervisors ignore behavior that should be given attention? Are the employees set up to compete against one another? What is the emotional health of your workplace? If you look at the larger picture, you can achieve a clearer, more informed view as to how to tackle it. Is there someone whom you trust that will listen to you with openness and honesty? Though you are the victim of the bullying, are you willing to look at what part you play in the dynamic? This is not a matter of excusing bullying but rather taking stock in how your reaction to it can help you to understand effective strategies to have it stop.

Just as important as identifying workplace bullying, is how to deal with the anger and move forward. If the bullying is taken care of, and you've been able to stay at your job, you may still experience anger around the issue. When you find yourself in a clear emotional state, that's the time to ask yourself, "Do I need to pursue this any longer? Did the bullying fit an old pattern of being ignored by superiors or parents? Do I have problems with authority?"

It might be a strange concept when you've been bullied, but this negative situation can actually be one of the greatest gifts in your life, because it's going to give you an opportunity to look at the dynamic of bullying. Bullies are very insecure people, and that's why they become bullies. It's very important for them to feel superior to other people. Very often they will pick on strong people in order to take them down. When I say strong, I mean people who are confident in what they do and how they do it. The bullies will always seem to pick them out. You are probably good at your job, which could show weakness in a boss that lacks confidence. The most important thing is to take appropriate action. Often that means putting the abuse in writing as a formal, legal complaint so that you will be due a response. When the bullying is not addressed, and you are in a position to leave the environment, you have to tap into your self-worth and leave, knowing that you took positive action.

RELATIONSHIPS & FAMILY BULLYING

Bullying rears its head in romantic and family relationships. Very few people have not experienced some level of being bullied. The dynamics of close relationships evoke both the best and the worst in people! When there are emotions involved, and we create a history with one another, there will be times when someone exerts power over a person close to them. Love, expectation, interconnection, stress, closeness, and dependency are just some of the wide-ranging feelings - both positive and negative - in partnerships and families that can lead to an imbalance. Bullying is the opposite of harmony between people. As we know, it's unrealistic to think we'll be in relationship/

family bliss all of the time, but bullying must be recognized and resolved.

Bullying can include belittling, bossiness, putting down, discounting feelings or opinions, etc. Some people know all too well how a parent's bullying can affect them for life. Inflicting emotional guilt from a parent is especially harmful, even if delivered subtly. In its most severe form, physical abuse is part of bullying. It's so important for us to be aware of our own situations as we witness others being bullied. Don't ignore signs. Don't think that the red flags you observe or feel are in your imagination. Talk to someone and get perspective.

Standing up for yourself to a partner or family member can be tricky. We worry about the relationship and - if the bully has been effective as a bully - they have worn down your judgment and self-preservation. Above all, take back your power. At first, that's the power to define the bullying and acknowledge its presence. You must do this before you start working to combat it, for you'll gain deeper vision of what you need to do to stop the bullying and begin to heal. Ultimately, removing ourselves from a relationship, or ceasing contact with a family member may be the best way to truly move forward if other options are impossible.

CYBERBULLYING

Cyberbullying has opened up a floodgate for abuse, with serious potential for harm. For all the wonderful benefits of the Internet and social media, the flip side is that people are going after one another online, hiding behind the technology which allows for an easier, removed, distant form of aggression. Things get said on social media that most people would have a very hard time saying to someone's face. Often, the cyberbullies have no personal relationship with their target. No one is immune. Posting an opinion becomes an invitation for bullies to descend. False accusations, vicious attacks, and insults can become what feels like a campaign with devastating effects. As someone once said to me, a blank screen or paper never refuses ink, and these days, *anybody* can say *anything* about you.

Kids and teens are the most vulnerable when it comes to cyberbullying. As mentioned above, cases of teen suicide often have a bullying component and at least some, if not all, of that bullying occurs online. We are in a new world and we are struggling with the tools to handle it. More is being done to attempt to deal with cyberbullying. Laws are beginning to address the phenomena, parental controls are available, information and anti-bullying programs in schools are focusing on the role of social media. Technology experts are working on things that might help like filters for bullying-type language on Facebook and other outlets that could ask a user who is about to post an offending message if they really want to go ahead and post, then making them wait a minute before they do. The research shows that this cuts down on aggressive messages. There is so much more to do in an environment that seems to be running away with itself, with new apps and modes of digital communication constantly developing.

Cyberbullying is faceless and seemingly out of control. If you know that someone is being bullied online, speak up, do what you can to get to the root of it, and most importantly, make sure the child, teen or adult who is being bullied has support. It can be nearly impossible for someone - especially a teen who is trying to figure out their identity and longs for social acceptance - to see the bigger picture beyond the cyber abuse. In the case of a minor, you can limit the use of the technologies and try your best to report the bullying. We need to look at the limitations of what people can do to one another under the guise of free speech. It is a very hard line to draw in order to protect everyone's rights, but we are at a crossroads as a global society. The language that we use with one another has become so tainted, cruel and cowardly. We hear and read so much of it, that many are becoming numb to it. This is very dangerous. Bullies can gain power over us in a way we didn't see coming if we don't wake up.

Bullies are not confident people. Their whole energy is about making sure they bring you down to a level below them so they feel good about themselves – temporarily. The bullying usually continues because they have to constantly boost their confidence. The Internet is a welcoming stage for this. I like to say there are two types of "net." There's the Internet, which is open to both good things and abuse, and there's the Inner-net, which you should be using to catch anything that shouldn't be in your life and look at it closely. It's better to be on the Inner-net than it is to be on the Internet! Blocking the bully from sending you email or messages on social media is an effective step, but more has to be done to shine a light on why people do this to one another, and how to help and heal, especially those who are particularly vulnerable. Further into these pages, I will address some practical steps you can take, both externally and through the use of mindful thought and attitude.

Show me a bully and I'll show you someone who has probably been bullied themself. When we work to stop bullying it can have a positive effect moving forward to stop the chain of abuse. A bully is suffering in some way, whether from past hurts or an inability to believe in themselves without putting someone else down. A bully doesn't feel complete on their own terms. They may have a strong exterior and project confidence, but inside they are unsure of who they are and their potential without taking power away from someone else. A bully is usually an unhappy person. They could feel alone, vulnerable, or scared. The bullying could come from their past, or be directly tied to a recent disappointing or painful event or situation in their lives. You need to take care of yourself and others - especially in the case of children being targeted for bullying, but the bully also needs help. Try to be mindful of that.

GETTING HELP, TAKING ACTION, AND TRANSFORMING YOURSELF

Bullying should never be ignored. There are different ways to go about taking action and getting help, but if bullying isn't recognized and dealt with, it will only get worse. Often the person being bullied, especially a child, is not in a position to change the dynamic. That is why parents must be aware, notice signs, and take careful, well-thought-out steps to support their kids and do something about the bullying. Many adults are not able to affect the change they need when they are being bullied. We must learn to reach deep inside ourselves and stand up for what is right.

If the victim of the bullying is someone else in your life, you can gently help them to gain an objective view of what is happening to them, and begin to take action. It can start with reaching out, encouraging and complimenting them. Bullying takes a toll on self-confidence, the very kind of confidence someone needs to stand up to the bully. That's the very loop of abuse and declining self-worth that the bully counts on.

There's a lot of evil and ill will in our world. We can work on healing our planet by acts of support, caring, and kindness with the people around us. Whether it is your child, a friend, or even a stranger standing in line with you at a movie theater, how we treat one another on a micro-level reverberates out to the universe. Bullying, cruelty, rudeness, and dismissiveness are too often accepted or brushed aside. Good people must embody the opposite spirit and help whoever they can. Evil is not going away, but goodness and positivity, the opposite side of the pendulum, has to be nurtured. When we fight back against bullying, we help our world.

With children or teens who are the victims of bullies, communication is key. You must make sure you are listening to your child, and be careful not to project your own feelings and experiences on to theirs. If a memory of a past episode of having been bullied is triggered, try not to convey fear or anger. Ask the right questions of your child: who is doing the bullying, where, how often, who else is there, etc. Be sensitive to the fact that a parent getting involved can sometimes make things worse. This is one of the major challenges and a very thin line to travel. Obviously, if your child is in danger, you must act and act quickly.

Be aware that even bullying that seems low-key can have a devastating effect on your child. Try to get as much information as you can. Decide what actions you need to take. What can you do for your child in terms of their feelings and confidence? Learn how to navigate the outreach that is available. Speak to your child's school. Do not go it alone if you need support in creating a plan of action that stops the bullying.

You can help your child by talking to them about trying to be able to see the bully as someone who is suffering in a way that has manifested as cruelty to others. Explain how negative feelings that are not expressed in a healthy way can turn into bullying. The bully is in emotional pain and probably very insecure. By putting someone else down, they feel superior, although only temporarily. A child can try to avoid being in harm's way by being with others and not where the bully will be able to victimize them easily. At times it's fitting for your child to respond to a bully with kindness, though often it's more appropriate for them to just walk away. Each situation is different. You can help your child build the skills to decide.

Cyberbullying can be hidden and insidious, often requiring extra attention. It's impossible to know what exactly is going on with your child, especially if they are a teen. With this and other forms of bullying, it is vitally important that schools do something about it. Some schools have recognized this growing problem and have begun to implement policies and programs to combat it. Other schools are slower to act. Speak to the principal. If the principal of the school doesn't do something about it, you need to point out their negligence which is both a moral and legal issue.

I hope that in the near future ALL schools have their priorities and resources geared toward addressing the issue of bullying and cyberbullying. There are many successful programs, many are worked into the curriculums with the intention of educating students and making them aware of consequences *before* there is an incident, rather than after. Of course we cannot stop all bullying, but schools working with parents can reduce bullying and raise children's awareness of the value of kindness and caring towards one another.

When you yourself are the victim of a bully, you are being given an opportunity for your own self-reflection and transformation. That may be a difficult concept to wrap your head around, but real change is possible when you find your inherent power and stand up for yourself. Whether or not the bully changes is not important.

You have to get it into your head that you are in control, you have to make decisions, and you must stand by your decisions. This can cause a lot of anxiety for some people, but try to tap into your courage and quiet the self-critical voice in your head. When you stand up for your rights, you'll be able to access what belongs to you, not the bully. As an example, if someone's bullying includes yelling at you, you can remember that the yelling belongs to the person doing it, not you.

When someone is yelling, or speaking to you harshly, they are telling you that they are in a state of heightened emotion, or anger. They probably lack the tools or self-awareness to calm their anger. You are given a chance in this scenario to think about what it means to have someone angry with you. Take time to look at your childhood. Were you often accused of something that you didn't do, or the target of misplaced rage or unhappiness? If someone's anger with you puts you in a state of fear or reprisal, look at your childhood. You may want to seek help with a trained professional to find the root cause of memories that trigger fear in your adult life and make you more sensitive and susceptible to the hurt that bullies can create.

Trying to talk to a bully can be very difficult. They can manipulate your attempts to reach out or try to appeal to your feelings. When somebody is sending bad energy your way, you could saturate them with love. They might change, but they might not, in which case they will probably disappear from your life because they won't be able to stand the light. You only cast a shadow when you're in the presence of a greater light. YOU can be the greater light. Let the bully's shadow arise and with that, the possibility of healing for everyone.

Be aware of not just overt bullying, but subtle bullying also. An example of that is a friend who always cancels their plans with you or treats you differently than other friends. Or a parent who disapproves of you by their silence, or a boss who overlooks you for a promotion, again and again. When you're being bullied you have an opportunity to break through and become an extremely strong person who can spot even the subtlest of bullying that's going on around you. When you empower yourself you will also be driven to help people who are being bullied.

Don't forget that you are in control of your own life. Affirmations such as, "I am worthwhile, I am wonderful, I am loving," can help you break through. Children can be taught affirmations also, which can be useful when they walk into school or are in settings where they feel vulnerable. As difficult as bullying is, while you're working on the solution that fits your situation best, try to stay positive and be true to yourself. Know that there is always help out there if you ask for it. Don't be afraid to ask!

By asking for help we find ourselves becoming even more and more powerful. Reach out for help from the right source. A close friend or family member can be the first person to approach, along with therapists, teachers, and counselors. The unconscious effect of bullying is not one to take lightly. Even if you've moved on, and the bullying took place years ago, you could still be dealing with the fallout in terms of your sense of self-worth and maybe even attracting bullies into your life now.

Here are some practical tips we don't always think of when dealing with bullies:

- **Try to look at the bigger picture of the bullying**. What started it? Did something transpire that leads back to when it began? Bullying is unacceptable behavior, but by taking in all of the elements we can not only begin to possibly unravel the tension, but also gain understanding about ourselves when we recognize a vulnerability that made us a target.
- **Deal with your feelings**. When you bottle up the hurt you experience from bullying, you only increase the likelihood it will continue. If you identify as a victim, you will be one. Recognize your feelings, discuss them with someone you

trust, learn from these emotions, and then let them go.

- **Find courage and bravery, even when you feel put-down and fragile.** When you are in fear or panic, you cannot make good decisions or take proper care of yourself. Bullies seize on what they perceive to be weakness. Project as much strength as you can. Challenge the bully's behavior in a non-aggressive way.
- **Operate from a place of compassion, calmness, and kindness, whether directly to the bully, or just in spirit if you are not going to have any communication with them**. When people are treated with respect, everyone benefits. If the bully's words and actions are contrary to this, you don't have to stoop to their level. Look at the way you react to the bully. Resist the urge to lash out. Remain grounded and secure.

CHANGING THE ENVIRONMENT

We see the spirit of bullying reflected in both the small scale of individual people's experiences, and in events across the globe. How do we change the environment of intolerance into the atmosphere of acceptance and recognition, improving our world for the better? There's been an acceptance of cruel behavior that needs to stop. People must take responsibility for the way we treat one another, whether we know them or they are strangers who live on the other side of the map.

You don't know where the bullying is going to come from, or what form it's going to take. Sometimes, when other strategies are not practical, or when it is not worth confronting the bully, you can look toward changing your environment. You can report the behavior and seek help but you do not have to put yourself in situations that harm you. Standing up to a bully doesn't have to involve a face to face experience. Move toward others who are supportive and positive. Do not isolate yourself. Find safe places and people. Take yourself off of social media (and help kids who are being bullied to avoid it.)

It's important to try and understand what it is that's driving the bully. They're probably feeding on your fear. They thrive on breaking you down and taking away your confidence. Changing the environment can have far-reaching meaning, beyond the physical space we might want to avoid if we are being bullied there. It can mean changing the environment of your thinking, about yourself and others. It speaks to viewing events and your place in them with a different lens. When you change the environment inside of yourself, the definition of who you are shifts and opens up to new possibilities.

When adults - and kids - are being bullied, they often hear the advice "just ignore it." As well meaning as those words can be, it is usually not effective to ward off the feelings that come in the aftermath of bullying. Dealing with it from the outside (reporting it to a teacher, supervisor, or the law as applicable, getting outside help, talking directly and calmly to the bully - if possible and practical) *and* the inside (processing your feelings, learning to let them go, and finding compassion and empathy beyond the hurt) are going to be the most effective approaches.

Be aware of the company you keep. Your most important company is yourself and the voice in your head - the one that tells you, you are good, bad, ugly, stupid, brilliant, etc. can be very powerful, in both a positive and negative way. You are manifesting everything and your mind is creating your reality. You are in control, your satsang (your company) starts with you, then goes out to the people around you. Who are the people around you right now? What type are you attracting into your life right now? The company that you keep will indicate the kind of people that you attract into your life. Change your environment by inviting in people who will relate to who you are and will understand what gifts you bring to the table. You want to be in the company of people who compliment the essence of who you are!

THE ROLE OF THE SUBCONSCIOUS

Master Your Own Mind

No one is to blame for being bullied, but it is both helpful and a tremendous opportunity to look into our subconscious. We attract into our lives what's hidden in our unconscious mind. There is a saying that goes, "That which you feared the most has come upon you." When we look at our fears, we learn a lot about ourselves. We can begin to unravel why we feel the way we do about ourselves. When you change your energy, you will notice things around you also change, perhaps even the bullying.

Did you see one parent bullying the other parent when you were a child? Were you bullied at a critical time in your development toward forming your identity? Look back into the circumstances of your story and see if you are bringing those patterns into your current daily life. The same is true if you are the one who bullies other people. Along with self-reflection and meditation, therapy is very useful. There are many methods and tools to connect with your subconscious and view the bullying through a more complex and revealing lens. As difficult as bullying can be – and potentially scarring – it can be an invitation to explore inward, for both healing and self-understanding.

There are always three ways to look at your life: 1) who you are, 2) who others see you as, and 3) who you really are. Only you know who you really are. Most people don't know their true self. They're terrified to look; afraid they won't like who they see! In some cases, people have buried who they really are very deep inside of themselves. When an event happens in your life, take time and see if there are any hidden messages in what occurred that you may have overlooked. Your unconscious sees more information, usually over time. Have you ever been in a situation where you were misunderstood? Did you feel someone judged you unfairly? Was there a time when someone's opinion was projected onto you and you were painted in a way that didn't actually reflect your true self? This happens all the time, to everyone. Remember, all perception is projection. We are constantly projecting our "stuff" onto other people. Bullying is a prime example.

The mind holds all the answers within. That is its magic. We have to look at how we access that magic by processing the subconscious, which is driven by our past experiences, and learn how to speak to ourselves in a positive, reinforcing way. Are the voices in your head critical? Are you helping the bully who is trying to put you down? The voice in your head has to be engaged and you must learn to listen and trust your gut feelings. The bully tries to take this from you. When you need to speak up and/or do something about the bullying, you'll need to know who you are and believe in that person.

Be kind to yourself, always, and talk to your mind with kindness. That is how we begin to master our mind. Make the choice today to realize there are enough people out there to criticize you without you doing it to yourself. The most important company that you keep is in your head. The people you are drawing into your life are not so much there to hurt you, but to show you the unresolved issues in your mind. Pay attention to self-criticism, try to speak to yourself in positives. It's helpful to begin your morning with affirmations that you can call upon throughout the day.

When you are the target of bullying, it can be difficult to remember to look inside of yourself for strength and wisdom. The bully can set the tone but you need to reject the label of "victim" and see the value in shifting your perspective. Accept your feelings, then try to let go of the labels that others - and you - have given to yourself. Change your mantra! When an event happens, remember, there are only really two answers to it - a negative one and a positive one. You're wired to be attracted to pleasure and averted by pain. As long as you keep stepping into the negative, it's going to keep showing up wearing a different overcoat, a different set of clothes, a different set of circumstances. Be open to what a difficult situation or experience can bring you once you have worked through it, taken whatever action is appropriate, looked within, and mastered your own mind.

DO YOU FEAR YOUR OWN POWER?

Bullying is about using fear to have power over someone. True power is something that lies within you, and not with anyone who would use bullying as a tactic to get what they want or to feel superior. The problem of bullying is so prevalent in our world, as bullies take advantage of the fact that many people fear their own power and energy. Bullies can only feel powerful when they are trying to take someone else's power away.

Set aside some time to work on the following questions, perhaps writing your responses down for further reflection later:

- Is it your own power or somebody else's power that you fear the most?
- What does power mean to you? Did you feel that a teacher was more powerful

than you? Did you feel that the police were more powerful than you? Did you feel that your parents were more powerful than you? Did you watch your mother control your father? Did you watch your father control your mother?

- Do you see power as something to be shared, or as something to control other people with? Take a moment and form a picture of what power means to you. What does it look like? What does it feel like? When you recall these pictures, are they positive pictures or negative pictures?
- What is fear? In what ways have you felt fearful in your life? Is there a difference in your mind between fear and power? Or are they connected to each other?

What a lot of people don't understand is that fear is nothing but a lack of faith. If you have faith that you are good enough, worthy of happiness and strong, nothing can stand in your way. If you have faith, you actually understand that whatever is meant for you will happen - both positive and negative. This is different than deserving good or bad; it means that both will come to you.

With bullying, and other challenges we face from people's behavior, we can take action, care for ourselves, and even gain a depth of experience that we can perhaps share with others, helping them through their own experiences. But we cannot control what others do, or what events arise for us. The only thing we have power over is ourselves and our minds, and that power is the strongest force of all. We try our best to get away from anything that's painful, but if you don't face the pain you'll never tap into your own power.

It is not the event that's important, but how you react. Whether we like it or not, unpleasant events are going to happen.

Have faith that the Universe is running the show - not you. You can take external actions against a bully, but in your mind for the sake of feeling your own power, sit for as long as you can in the middle. Don't beat yourself up when things don't go as planned. The only way to know if you're progressing is when you are tested. Events will manifest to test your calmness. Every experience that has scarred you in your life is your greatest gift, if you choose to make it so. That's the real treasure - not a house, a car or the other possessions. They're all illusions that pass through your life. What's real about you are your battle scars.

Fear is not who we are, individually or as a planet. We are greater than fear. Fear is just the moment when we lose sight of ourselves. We are the creators of our own destiny. Fear devastates our lives, keeps us in a mental prison, and is the root cause of most illness. If you can let go of fear, you can have a happier, healthier and more productive life. Real faith is when you stand up for yourself and your own truth, even if you are going to walk away from a bully. It is a process that happens inside of you. No one can take that away from you.

ARE YOU A BULLY?

One of the most important things we can do when addressing the issue of bullying is to take a look at ourselves to examine whether we are ever the source of bullying behavior. When we see all the ways that bullying can rear its head, and how we might unwittingly be participating in it, we become more tuned in, able to change, and equipped to help one another.

Here are some questions to ask yourself:

- Do I anger quickly, lashing out before I've had time to think about my reaction?
- Do I tend to make threats, however subtle, or feel that someone needs to fear me in order to get what I want?
- Do I need to feel that I'm the one in

control in relationships, family and/or work situations?

- Instead of talking about my emotions - such as being unhappy in a relationship, or feeling slighted at work - do I act out in a negative way?
- Would I rather be right than have to admit I've made a mistake?
- Have I ever stopped communicating with someone without their understanding of what prompted my silence?
- Do I avoid topics that make me uncomfortable by shutting down other people?
- Am I dismissive of people who I feel are not worth my time and attention? Do I ignore people who want to talk to me about something that is bothering them?
- Do I respond to people who say "hello" to me, or smile, with a similar greeting?
- Do I avoid certain people in an obvious

way (leaving a room when they enter or changing my seat at a table?)

- Do I exclude people from conversations and/or dismiss what they are saying?
- Do I feel I have to protect myself from being hurt in certain situations by projecting an unemotional persona that may seem condescending or snobbish?
- What is my definition of "strength" in relationships? Am I afraid of appearing "weak?"
- Do I make hurtful statements to people on social media that I would never say face to face? Do I get into a lot of online arguments or heated debates where I attack or insult people?

If we can access our behavior in a gentle but honest way, we not only learn more about ourselves, but can start to shift the way we interact with one another. When we bully people, no matter how subtly, we contribute to a dynamic that has real repercussions. The hurt we cause may not be perceivable, but it's real. We are hurting ourselves also. Though we cannot solve all the bullying that goes on in our world, we can begin by looking in the mirror.

We need to treat everyone with kindness, even when we have a problem with them. Bullying never has a place at the table. I like to say that you don't have to always be obliging, but you have to speak obligingly. In other words, you don't have necessarily do what people ask, but you have to be kind to them no matter what. "Kindness costs nothing" is something to always remember. For bullies, kindness costs them their ego and their need to be right.

If you bully someone, you are hurting yourself just as much as you are potentially hurting them. We are meant to help one another, not harm. The best prayer for humanity is, "How may I help? What can I do? What have I got to offer? How can I demonstrate it?" I believe that what goes around, comes around. If you say something bad about another person, sooner or later somebody's going to say something bad about you. We reap what we sow.

It can be very difficult to admit to yourself that your child or teen is partaking in bullying behavior. You might see it firsthand, or learn about it when another parent or the school informs you. This is a serious issue that has to be addressed. Sticking your head in the sand, denying your child is bullying someone, is going to cause damage to everyone involved. Though you may want to defend your child, it's important that you take a balanced, fair look at the situation and get to the root of it if your child is victimizing someone. Cyberbullying in particular, can be very dangerous between teens. Social media can be amazingly valuable, but when used for bullying, it becomes a powerful weapon.

When your child is the bully, confront it right away, but also seek support and advice while holding them responsible. Make sure the target of your child's bullying and their parents know that you are aware and taking action. Be direct and honest with your child about the repercussions of their bullying. Look at what may be causing the bullying. Is something going on in their lives, or in the family, that could be triggering the behavior? Inquire about getting your child/teen help to process what they are doing and why.

Remember, we are given opportunities to confront situations and make changes. If you are a bully, or if your child is, it's the recognition and self-contemplation that can shift you or your child's actions into real transformation and growth. The same is true when you are the target of bullying, as painful as it can be. It's especially difficult to see our children go through this. It's all about attitude, support and kindness. No matter how bullying might be touching your life right now, it has to be addressed and processed. There is a gift in the struggle and a way to move with positivity through our greatest challenges.

MEDITATIONS & EXERCISES

When we are experiencing bullying, or even if we are not currently and just want to contemplate a more peaceful world, there are ways to work helpful thoughts into meditations or mindfulness exercises. There is also a lot of stress connected to bullying that can be lessened with meditation.

One of the simplest methods is to just take a deep breath, exhale, close your eyes, and ask your mind a question. A simple question that you want clarity about. As we go about our day, life presents so much noise and distraction. It's difficult to focus on something we want to look into more deeply with serenity. At first when you meditate on a question, you may find that hundreds (or more!) bits of information seem to stream through. Allow this to happen. As you continue to let your mind settle, you'll begin to get information that shines through and arises from the clutter. It may lend perspective on what's happening to you, or insight into a person who is bullying you, or alleviate harmful feelings you may be attributing to yourself, or reveal what your fears are truly about.

When you are confronting bullying, or taking an action related to it, make sure you are staying true to yourself. It can help to take three deep breaths before you say anything. This can help you to not react too quickly. When we are triggered, we can sometimes react in a way that would have been better served with some thoughtful calmness and objectivity. The worst time to communicate with other people is when emotions are running in your mind. Whether your feelings are positive or negative, it's important to have the ability to balance them. We can also look at our part in the dynamic. There's no excuse for bullying, but through it, the process of self-knowledge and evaluation is helpful.

When you need to look deeper into yourself to gain the strength to face a situation, it can be very helpful to go to a space where you can remain quiet for a period of time. Light a candle, take your deep breaths, and then close your eyes and just allow yourself to follow your breath. Think about a time when you felt really good about yourself. It might be a time when you helped someone or had a breakthrough that boosted your self-confidence. You will find that if the "company you keep" in your head is negative, you can begin to change it with this meditation. From this same type of meditation, we can also send a sense of kindness and even love to the bully, for they are probably suffering more than us. Whether in a meditation or just in your daily life, try to start talking to yourself in positive terms. Be careful of your thoughts. That voice that tells you you're not good enough needs to be corrected.

There are five principles of spirituality that can be very helpful as we apply it to the topic of bullying:

- The first principle - Every person you encounter is the right one. This means that no one comes into your life by chance. Everyone around us, and with whom we interact, has a defined purpose, whether to teach us something, or to help us cope with a current situation.
- The second principle - Whatever happens is the only thing that could have happened. None of what we experience, in every detail, could have been any other way. There is no, "if only I had done this differently, then it would have been different." What happened has happened and there should be no regrets.

- The third principle - Everything that happens in your life begins at exactly the right moment, neither too early nor too late. When you are ready, something new will come into your life.
- The fourth principle - What is over, is over. It is that simple. When something in our life ends, it helps our evolution. That is why we are enriched by every experience we have. It is better to let go of the past, as much as possible, and move on to the future.
- The fifth principle - Nothing is permanent. This is the universal truth. Everything will change; some sooner, some later. Change is inevitable. Once we understand and accept this, life becomes simpler. Letting go of anticipation and expectations, learning to be good to yourself, and loving with your whole being, is the way to be happy.

RESOURCES

The following is a list of websites that provide information and support for bullying, in all of its various forms. Please reach out for help when you are being bullied, or when you want to learn more about bullying's impact in our world.

stopbullying.gov

pacerkidsagainstbullying.org/kab/

abusergoestowork.com

bullying.co.uk

antibullyingireland.com

ABOUT THE AUTHOR

For more than 20 years, Derek O'Neill has been transforming the lives of thousands of people around the world for the better. An internationally acclaimed transformational coach and therapist, motivational speaker, author, martial arts sensei and humanitarian, Derek inspires and uplifts people from all walks of life through his workshops, consultations, speaking engagements, media, and tireless humanitarian work.

Drawing on thirty years of training in martial arts, which earned him the level of Master Black Belt, coupled with his extraordinary intuitive abilities and expertise as a psychotherapist, Derek has pioneered a new psychology, transformational therapy. His signature process, aptly named "The Sword and the Brush," helps clients to seamlessly transmute their struggles into positive outcomes, using the sword to cut away old patterns and the brush to help paint the picture of the new life that they require.

In addition to reaching large audiences through workshops and media, Derek advises individuals, celebrities, business leaders, and politicians, helping them to find new perspectives on long-standing issues and bringing harmony back to their lives and businesses.

Author of More Truth Will Set You Free, the Get a Grip series of pocket books, a cutting edge book on parenting titled Calm Mama,

Happy Baby, and several children's books, Derek also hosted his own radio show, "The Way With Derek O'Neill," which enjoyed the most successful launch in VoiceAmerica's history, quickly garnering 100,000 listeners.

Derek is a master at offering practical wisdom and proven techniques for living a more harmonious and fulfilling life, bringing CEOs to the level of wise yogi and wise yogis to CEO; he has worked with executives from some of the world's major airlines, and the cast of Spiderman on Broadway to help transform group disharmony and untapped creative potential into productivity and dynamic performance. He has been featured in Exceptional People Magazine, The Irish Independent, The Irish Examiner, CBS television, and RTE, Ireland's national TV network.

Inspired by his worldly travels, he formed SQ Foundation, a not-for-profit organization focused on helping to solve global issues facing humanity today. In 2012, he was honored as Humanitarian of the Year and named International Celebrity Ambassador for Variety International the Children's Charity. He was welcomed as Vice President of the esteemed charity in May 2013.

Recordings of Derek's discourses are available for download, offering practical wisdom and proven techniques for living a more harmonious and fulfilling life.

To learn more about Derek O'Neill, to attend his next workshop, to order books, downloads or to contact him, please visit his website:

derekoneill.com

To learn more about SQ Foundation, the global charity that is changing the lives of hundreds of thousands of people around the world, go to:

sq-foundation.org

MORE RESOURCES FROM DEREK O'NEILL

Get a Grip Book Series

Abundance: Starts Right Now

Addiction: What a Cover-Up!

Anger: Who Gives a Shite?

Bullying: You Won't Beat Me

Confidence: Easy For You to Say

Depression: What's that?

Dreams: The Best Messengers

Excellence: You Never Lost It, You Forgot It

Fear: A Powerful Illusion

Forgiveness: So I Can Move On

Gratitude: Yes Please

Grief: Mind Boggling But Natural

Happiness: You Must Be Effin' Joking!

Mindfulness: Out Of Or In Your Mind?

Relationships: Would You Want to Date You?

Stress: Is Stress Stressing You Out?

Suicide: Fast or Slow

Weight: What's Eating You?

Other Books

More Truth Will Set You Free

Calm Mama, Happy Baby

Children's Books

Water Drop Coloring Book

The Adventures of Lucinda in Love-Filled Fairyland

SOCIAL MEDIA

YouTube

youtube.com/DerekONeill101

Facebook

facebook.com/DerekONeill101

Twitter

twitter.com/DerekONeill101

LinkedIn

linkedin.com/in/DerekONeill101